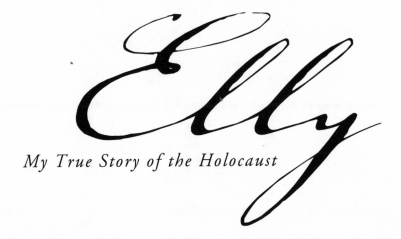

My True Story of the Holocaust

Elly

My True Story of the Holocaust

an

her

ob

w can I find you?... She never find the

he Sue flew from tree   tree, one day she found

el   y wounds and torn feather

wo   unded birds   a fall tre

t which stood in spite of heavy rain a

y remember those birds   the heavy storm

y that   with th

er

Elly Berkovits Gross

SCHOLASTIC PRESS/NEW YORK

(Back) Childhood image of author from the collection of Elly Berkovits Gross

Interior: Photos 1, 2, 3, 13, 14, 15, 16 from the collection of
Elly Berkovits Gross; Photo 4 (freight car) © Ira Nowinski/CORBIS;
Photo 9 (suitcases) © Nathan Benn/CORBIS; Photo 11 (factory
interior) courtesy of Volkswagen AG; Photo 12 (Ebensee) ©
US Army Photograph/SODA. The following photos courtesy of
Państwowe Muzeum Auschwitz-Birkenau: 5,6: photographs by
Stainslaw Luczko 1945; 7: SS photograph 1944; 8: SS
photograph 1941; 10: SS photograph 1944

Library of Congress Cataloging-in-Publication Data is available

ISBN-13: 978-0-545-07494-0
ISBN-10: 0-545-07494-0

Originally published in part as *Storm Against the Innocents*

12 11 10 9 8 7 6 5 4 3 2 1   9 10 11 12 13

Printed in the U.S.A.   23
First Scholastic Hardcover printing, March 2009

Book design by Susan Schultz
Display text set in Johanna Sparkling
Body text set in Adobe Garamond

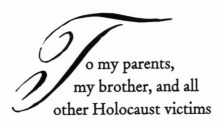

To my parents,
my brother, and all
other Holocaust victims

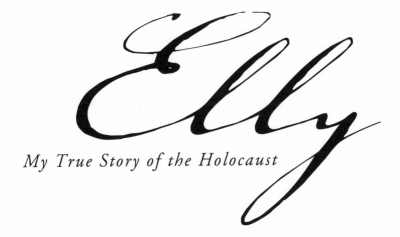

My True Story of the Holocaust

Foreword

ELLY GROSS, MY MOTHER

My mother had me soon after she returned from the concentration camp. She was fifteen when the Hungarians and Germans took her away. She came home after the terrible ordeal to find her parents and her brother gone. She returned to her home to find it occupied by strangers, who proceeded to chase her away.

Mom dreamed of going to school, but she needed to find a home. She met my dad, who was eight years older, and got married. She skipped her teenage years; she never had time to develop into an adult. She struggled together with her husband, also a survivor, to forget and to start a new life.

My father was a farmer before the war, but when the Communists took over, he had to give his land to the collective and take a government job in the next village. He was always at work, and Mom was lonely and kept me close to her. I was her ray of sunshine, her beautiful little bright doll, the doll she was unable to have as a child. She spoiled me. I got the best toys my parents could afford, the only tomato in the house, the prettiest clothes that could be found. At the same time, Mother wanted me to be strong, to know about life. She wanted me to read at four, learn to sew at five, and be able to cook when I was six. I was sick a lot, and our village did not have a doctor. The school had only four grades, which were taught by one teacher in one large room. Mom was determined to move to the city, where there were better schools and good medical care, but the Communist Party forbade anyone to move there unless he or she had a house and a job. After my brother was born and I once again became ill, Mother somehow managed to get a job in the city. We moved to the house my parents were building there, but only one room was finished. Dad had to stay behind for another year until he was able to get a job as well. I always remember Mother striving to achieve her goals and never taking "no" for an answer if there was any stone left unturned.

I don't remember at what age I became aware of the horrible ordeal my parents had gone through during the Holocaust or at what age I saw the first book describing those horrible experiences. I just know that at some point in my life my mother showed it to me and explained why she did not have her parents or her brother. It was a while before I understood that she felt guilty because she was unable to save her young mother.

Mother had a few friends. They were all survivors and all older than her, because she was one of the youngest who survived the camps. I was amazed that all these survivors managed to function, have children, go to the theater, care about life, after the ordeal they went through.

There was always the shadow of anti-Semitism around us. Our house had to be spotless, our appearance had to be neat. We did not want to literally be "dirty Jews." I also felt the need to make amends for my parents. I needed to help around the house, and I had to be a good student. They had suffered enough.

Later my family moved to the United States, and Mother went on to do the things that survivors do. Together with my father, she achieved the American dream. Mother got a high school education, helped my father build a business, buy a house and a car. Her children went to college and started successful careers. She had grandchildren who, in turn, went on to good colleges and are starting great careers. Mother got a college degree at the age of sixty-nine. She was the oldest in her classes.

Now she has found her purpose in life. She will not let people forget the atrocities. She will teach young people that prejudice of all kinds is wrong, teach that discrimination and violence are wrong. She went on the March of the Living with young people several times. She travels to schools all over the country to speak to students and writes books to convey her message.

My mother, Elly Gross, is not only a survivor; she is also an achiever.

— *Agneta Weisz*

Introduction

MIRACLES HELPED ME TO SURVIVE

I am convinced that my survival in the Holocaust is because of a chain of miracles. I do not consider myself special. But without those miracles, I would not have survived. I would have perished with all the other children of my age. I survived by these miracles:

I was blonde, with blue eyes and white skin. Hungarian law forbade Jews to travel. But every Sunday, I secretly traveled by train to Marghita to pick up food from an aunt and returned home to Şimleu Silvaniei at night. No one ever asked me, "Why are you traveling?"

In the ghetto of Cehei, which held more than seven thousand inhabitants, four were ordered to peel potatoes. I was one of them. I had plenty of raw or boiled potatoes to eat. Whenever we left the ghetto, we were strip-searched. I would hold my pocketknife tightly. I was never caught.

On arrival to Auschwitz-II/Birkenau, Dr. Mengele directed me to the right at the last second. Tragically, my mother and brother were not directed to the right.

In Auschwitz-II/Birkenau Block 20, my group stood in knee-high rainwater. Assisted by luck, I was transferred to Block 18 to be with my cousins. I passed out the next day at roll call, but an angel held out her wings. Dr. Mengele did not notice me. I was taken inside.

I ate potato peels mixed with sand from a garbage pile. It filled my empty stomach, but I did not get sick. My tummy was enlarged. At the next selection, Dr. Mengele pointed it out, but he let me go with others whose lives were spared.

In the factory, a German *Meister*[1] risked his freedom and brought me salt to stop my gums from bleeding. When I coughed and was ill with high fever, another miracle happened. Although I had a blanket on my back, a German officer didn't beat me for not obeying orders. I was sick and yet not shipped away. Because I was blonde?

While on the train returning home, a Russian soldier tried to drag me away. To him I looked German. Because I was blonde? I got away, and I hid under a bench, behind others' legs. No one on the train betrayed me. I escaped.

1. A factory supervisor.

By a chain of miracles, my life had been spared. One last miracle should have come, but it did not — if only another member of my family would have survived. I was alone. Both my parents and my brother had perished. There was no one to love and protect me, no one to provide a home for me.

— *Elly Berkovits Gross*

I WENT TO KINDERGARTEN

*W*ith a blue bow in my hair and a lunch bag in my hand, I went to kindergarten on a windy, cloudy day. As I approached the nursery, a little rain sprinkled. But I was not too wet as I walked down the long hallway. Another girl entered with an umbrella in her hand. My umbrella was at home. I felt desperate. Standing on my toes, I opened the door and ran out crying into the pouring rain to return home.

My parents' neighbor's son saw me on the rainy street. He asked, "Why are you crying? What's wrong?" Sobbing hysterically, I explained that one girl came with an umbrella to kindergarten. And I did not have one, so I had to return home to get my umbrella. He took me home in his arms.

I will never forget this episode as long as I live. How foolishly a child's mind works! I was already at school, yet I ran out crying into the rain and got soaking wet, just for an umbrella. Soon the rain stopped and the sun shone in the blue sky.

What a silly child I was. Mother changed my wet clothes. Smiling, she put me into bed, and I cried as I fell asleep.

My hometown

$\mathcal{I}$ remember Şimleu Silvaniei, Romania, where I was born, as a beautiful city. The city lies in a valley, surrounded by the Meses Mountains. All year round, there is snow on these mountains.

In the summer, when it rained or when the sun shone bright, some snow melted. The city's river, the Crasna, rapidly rose, overflowing its banks. Muddy water covered the left side of my hometown. People packed and moved to higher ground. The muddy water swept away everything in its path.

I lived on the right side of the river by the Magura Hills. From these high hills, a small stream with crystal-clear water flowed slowly down the middle of my street. In the center of the paved street in the summer's warm weather, my friends and I dammed the water with sand to create our own small lake. We floated our paper boats on the lake. Proud "sailors" made from matches navigated the boats on our lake. Those paper boats soaked and soon sank. The one whose boat went under first was the loser in that game.

Our fun ended when it rained or when more snow melted. The stream grew angry and big. Water covered our street from one side to the other, carrying stones and broken tree branches.

When it got cold, the water froze and created a frozen street from side to side. We children hurried to play on the ice. Our mothers worried that we would get frostbite. The cold never bothered us.

My only doll

Twice a year with Mother, we visited my grandmother. Granny lived in another town, so she seldom had a chance to see us. Her other seven grandchildren visited her almost daily. And as some grandmothers do, she criticized them for everything.

Grandmother loved me a lot, but she never gave me a gift. In the 1930s, few people could spend money on presents. Families could not buy gifts or toys. They were satisfied to make ends meet. We children created our toys from wild chestnuts, matches, beans, ropes, strings, wildflowers, and stones.

Once, when my friend's father traveled, he brought home doll furniture for my friend. Although my father always worked, he had no money for presents or toys. One time, my father took a trip, too, and he brought me back a beautiful doll. I was happy and felt like I was "in heaven." The doll had a porcelain face and blonde hair.

I ran to my friend with my new gift and suggested that we play with her doll furniture and my doll. She said, "Let me see your doll." I put my beautiful doll in her hand. Then she hit it on the side of a wood barrel and broke my only doll's nose. Devastated, I ran home crying. Mother said, "If you do not like that she broke your doll's nose, do not play with her anymore." Mother was smart!

The next day, we played together again. We tried to repair the doll's nose. My friend pretended to be a doctor, and I was a nurse. We could not repair the broken nose. I never got another doll.

MY FIRST DANCING CLASS

My aunt's younger brother opened a dancing school for teenagers. With a few of my friends, I registered for classes. We learned how to dance gracefully and not step on our partners' toes.

Some of my friends had prior dance instruction. For them, it was easy to follow the music and dance gracefully. At my first dance lesson, I was clumsy. Not many boys asked me for a dance.

My disappointment increased as heavy storm clouds darkened the sky. It thundered, and lightning hit the dance hall. Electric wiring short-circuited, and we were in complete darkness. Heavy rain with egg-size hail covered the ground.

I was scared and miserable. I started to cry hysterically, "Please, someone help me get home to my mother." But who wants to walk in a heavy storm with a crying girl?

During the storm, more than eight inches of hail came down and covered the ground. The storm knocked out trees, and electric and telephone lines. It was hazardous and difficult to walk on the ice-covered streets.

As the storm raged, no one danced and everyone's time was ruined. People shoveled hail for hours and made piles of ice.

Cold and icy day

In my hometown, winter begins around October. First, it's cold, rainy, and windy; then the rain freezes on the street. It's treacherous to walk on icy roads. It does not matter, in rain or cold — the freezing weather does not stop children from going to school.

Parents worry that their children might fall on the slippery paths. In dangerous weather, they walk their children to school. My father worried that I might fall, so he got ready to accompany me to school on one cold, rainy day.

Frozen rain created ice on streets. To protect me, my father held a cane in one hand and with his other held my hand. He balanced himself with his cane. Father slipped on the slippery ice and fell backward. He hit his back and head hard. I tried to help him to get up, but he was big and I was small.

Crying, I asked people for help, but few people were out walking. From the bakery across the street, someone came to help my father up from the icy, frozen street. Luckily, my daddy was only bruised.

With no escort, I finally got to school. Our teachers dismissed classes early. The sun smiled and melted the ice. Soon there was none left on the street.

My only brother

$\mathcal{I}$ was an only child and jealous of my friends who had a brother or a sister with whom to play. I felt small and alone. Then, when I was ten years old, my little brother, Adalbert, was born. He was handsome, with black hair, red cheeks, and black eyes. I was happy to have a brother.

I loved the little boy, and he liked to be with me. He took his first steps, balanced with his hands, and, with a smile, he ran into my arms. I felt so joyous that I cried. Adalbert was close to my heart. It gave me great satisfaction when our mother trusted my little brother to my care. I planned to go together with him to the park when he grew up, and up to the hills to pick wild strawberries, black-berries, and wildflowers for our mother. Our father also had plans for his only son's bar mitzvah and the school he would attend. Maybe Adalbert would be a doctor, or per-haps a lawyer, or a mechanic.

In the spring, when my brother was born, the Nazis invaded Czechoslovakia. The winds of the Second World War began to blow over our heads, but no one could have imagined what would follow next. Fate changed our family's life, and our dreams would not come true.

The storm that
struck Europe

*T*hose who were born in the late 1920s or in the 1930s missed the prior, worry-free life before the Second World War. But Europe's problems began much earlier, even before World War I. Many people died during that war, and life afterward was difficult. There was a depression. Whose fault was it? It was easier to blame a group of people.

Which nation could be blamed for everyone's difficult and harsh life? It must be a nation without a homeland, a group of people who have no country of their own. That nation would be an easy target, and the Depression could be blamed on these people. They had no country on Earth to call their own.

By blaming Jews in the 1920s and 1930s, a fanatical German leader, Adolf Hitler, united his countrymen.

The slogan "Kill the Jews" was music to the ears of the Nazis[1] and their collaborators. In the storm that swept through Europe, Jews were easy prey. They had no homeland. They had no refuge. In this storm, my people were robbed of their possessions and their lives.

1. Members of the National Socialist Workers' Party, a political party led by Adolf Hitler, who controlled Germany from 1933 to 1945. During the Second World War, the Nazis conquered most of Europe.

Hungarian invasion

People in Europe were suffering; everyone was struggling. Depression is like a locust that eats everything in its path. As after a fire, only bare ground remains. In the market, there was plenty of food, but few had money to buy it. No work. No income. But even though life was harsh, we were home together and we had our freedom.

Soon more problems arose. On September 10, 1940, the Hungarian takeover of my part of Romania brought devastation to the local inhabitants. The new government seized treasures, looted everything, and took control of the border. We were now part of Hungary.

Day by day, life got harder. Hungarians brought misery with them. Coupons were distributed. Food, clothing, and shoes were rationed. Jews were blamed for the lack of goods. The new government seized Jewish belongings and property and gave them away for free to loyal Hungarians.

Local Hungarians were happy for a while, but they got greedy and demanded more.

Harsh new laws hit Jews. Restrictions were issued for travel and schooling; curfews were implemented; men were drafted into forced labor and other injustices.

It was spring. It was warm. The sun was shining. Meadows were green. Trees and flowers were blooming, but it was dark and cloudy for Jews. To appease the locals and the Germans, the Hungarian government forced Jews out of their homes, out of their cities. Then they gave the Jews to the Nazis.

The tenant accused me

Mommy seldom had to repeat that I should listen to adults. I tried to please the elders so they would not scold me. One day, our tenant went to the market and bought two chickens. She placed them across from her home's entrance in a sort of box that had small openings. As always, cats and dogs ran around the small yard. Maybe one touched the opening to the box, so the chickens got out. The entrance to our apartment was on the other side of the building. I rarely used the back entrance. I did not even know that the lady had any chickens.

One late afternoon, the tenant called me and said, "You played with my chickens as if they were balls." Mommy came out and said, "Do not worry. I will pay for the chickens." She said this even though we did not have much money and she knew that I had been in school all day. My father had already been taken away to a forced labor camp.

Mommy knew I would not touch someone else's property. My dear mother was worried that this tenant might go to the police and complain about me. Then who knew what would happen? They could put me in jail. The tenant made a lot of noise and screamed that she even had a witness who had seen me play with the chickens.

I was so scared, trembling, ready to pass out. Then, from nowhere, the two chickens returned. They went back into the box from which they had escaped earlier. The three of us stood there. This unreliable woman didn't say, "Sorry that I accused you." She was a Hungarian, and we were Jews. Mommy said, "Thank goodness, the chickens returned. Who cares about an apology. Our worries are over."

This was our life under Hungarian rule.

MY DEAR DADDY

*M*y daddy was handsome, tall with black hair and black eyes. He loved me. Up to the age of ten, I was his only child, and I resembled his late mother. His mother had been pretty, with blue eyes, blonde hair, and a light complexion. At an early age, my daddy became an orphan. His father died in the First World War. Shortly after, his mother passed away.

The four handsome children remained in the care of their late father's brother. But this uncle sent the four boys away, and he took over their parents' house. The young boys traveled away from their village to find work. My daddy was fourteen years old, the eldest of the orphans. The four brothers learned tailoring, and their room and board was their salary.

Eventually, two of Daddy's brothers escaped their misery. They left for South America and settled in Montevideo, Uruguay, to start a new life in a strange land. The two brothers began to work, and then they opened a dry-cleaning store. My daddy's youngest brother soon followed the others to Uruguay. Now the three brothers were together, and Daddy was struggling in the old country. In Europe, there was a recession and no work. Then catastrophe fell on the European Jews.

My dear father was drafted into a forced-labor camp in June 1942. His group marched on foot with no food, water, shoes, or warm clothes. One day, his keepers forced the group into a trailer, locked the doors, and poured gasoline around the trailer. Then the soldiers put a match to the gasoline and burned the workers alive. My thirty-seven-year-old father was among the group of young men who died that day.

I forever missed my daddy, who, far from his family, suffered cold and hunger for months. And fire took my dear daddy's life.

Miss, did a star fall on you?

After the Hungarian takeover in September 1940, we Jews were deprived of citizens' rights. In 1944, the Hungarian government issued a decree that we Jews must wear a yellow Star of David. The local population now could recognize a fearful Jew from far away on the street.

Locals called to us, "Dirty Jew — did a star fall on you?" They spit on Jews, and some Jews were beaten. That I was born a Jew was a daily shame. Former friends asked, "Miss, did a star fall on you?" even though I was the same Jewish child with whom they had grown up and played for many years on our street.

From the front door of our home, we could see most of our street, which began at the city's center. On the left side of the street, built on a hill, is the Catholic church, which rises over the city. Its church bells rang day and night, four times per hour. It was so beautiful to hear.

Each morning, I looked at the church's clock tower so as not to be late for school. And I looked with worry down the street to see my former friends leave for their school. I no longer wished to encounter them.

One of my former so-called "friends" became a street agitator. He threw stones, called names, and attacked elderly Jews. A few times he spat on me, too. When I told my mother, she said, "You, darling, must learn not to complain."

A question remains: Did the Jewish leaders know about the laws that were being made against Jews? With each new day, Jews had fewer and fewer rights. No one ever will know how much our leaders knew.

The knife with

a

Mother-of-pearl handle

Sometime in the 1930s an uncle from Santiago, Chile (one of my mother's brothers) came to visit his birthplace to see his mother, sisters, brothers, and other relatives. He was a handsome bachelor, who planned to get married. Many families wished that perhaps he would choose their daughter. Friends recommended many girls. Finally, one day he found his match. His fiancée was chic and pretty. Granny was happy.

At the wedding, people danced on top of tables. The new couple sat me next to them and gave me two valuable presents: a narrow, two-inch knife with a mother-of-pearl handle, and a gold ring. The small knife came in handy on field trips organized by my school. As the lives of Jews in Europe became harder, the pocketknife became useful and indispensable.

Soon my life was changed forever. In early spring 1944, armed soldiers forced us out of our homes into a former brick factory outside of town. We now lived in this ghetto.[1] Then, on a sunny day, May 27, 1944, we were strip-searched in a tent. I hid the small knife by squeezing it in my hand.

We were forced into cattle cars without food or water—about ninety-five scared Jews: old men and women, young mothers with frightened hungry children. We had almost no air to breathe. In a corner, my mother, brother, and I were sitting between one another's legs. Then I began to make an airhole with my secret knife in the cattle-car wall.

On the next day, early Sunday morning, the cattle cars pulled into our hometown, into Șimleu Silvaniei, for the last time. It was another sunny day. The Hungarians came to the train station to see the locked cattle cars carrying the unfortunate Jews. The smiles and laughter on their faces are imprinted in my memory.

Late that night, our cattle cars left the city's station. I made the hole bigger in the cattle-car wall so that my mother, brother, and I had some fresh air. We were so desperate.

Adalbert, my five-year-old brother, asked for water and food. Our mother held him tight. Mommy kissed him. She had no food or water to give to her son, but at least we had some air.

1. A segregated, impoverished area of a city in which Jews were forced to live.

WHY I DID NOT SAY,
"MOMMY, PLEASE COME WITH ME?"

On Friday, June 2, 1944, the train suddenly halted and the doors were opened.

Men in striped rags jumped into our boxcar. One whispered to me, "Say you are eighteen," and to my mother, "Give the boy to someone." I thought, *Are these men lunatics?* The men pushed old people and children out of the cattle cars. The sick and dead were thrown together on the same truck. I thought, *What is wrong? Are they mad?*

Mother asked, "What should we do?" I said, "We cannot give my brother to strangers. He is five years old, and I am fifteen." It happened as fast as lighting; there was no time to think. I was pushed to the right.

My mother, holding my brother in her arms, remained on the left. As I ran to reach the others, I waved to them. They looked in my direction. I relive this moment all of my life. We had arrived at the Auschwitz-II/Birkenau concentration camp in Poland.

During my life, as problems arise, it crosses my mind that I made a terrible mistake. I am tormented with remorse. Why did I not say to my mother, "Give my brother to someone and come with me"? Why do I feel guilt that Mother was sent to the left?

In my life, tragedies poured on me. I was robbed of my father at age thirteen. When I was fourteen, he perished in a forced-labor camp. When I was fifteen, my mother and brother were taken from me. Was I selfish by not speaking up at that moment? By not saying, "Mommy, please come with me"? You, Reader, be the judge. Did I do wrong?

How did my mother die?

Our train with more than three thousand new deportees halted. Everyone was ordered to get out.

My dear mother thought that we would see our neighbor from down the street with her three girls. Mommy thought she would leave my brother in their care while we worked. In this turmoil, our neighbor was not found. We did not know where we were.

We were deceived. Everything happened as fast as lightning. My mother was holding my brother in her arms. Poor little boy, five years old, hungry, exhausted, had no strength to walk. But Adalbert did not cry. I was next to them. Someone pushed me away. I waved and ran to catch the few others directed to the right.

My mother and brother looked in my direction. I never saw them again. The other group in which my mother and brother remained grew larger. They were standing next to the cattle car in which we had traveled for seven days. No one with a normal mind could imagine their fate.

I always see my thirty-seven-year-old beautiful mother and my handsome five-year-old brother. I am tormented by how my dear ones were murdered.

Were my loved ones lucky to be killed in the gas chambers so they did not suffer too long? Many other adults and children were put to death even more cruelly. Who can tell me how my dear ones were killed? By a miracle, some of those who witnessed the massacre of European Jews survived. We who survived must tell our stories.

SYMPHONY MUSIC IN BIRKENAU

On arrival in Birkenau, Jews from all countries heard soft music. An orchestra played a symphony. The players wore striped rags. They were pale, but they played beautifully on their instruments. The players were well-known musicians in their respective countries.

When the musicians arrived in Auschwitz-II/ Birkenau, they were selected for a special task. Their music was supposed to mislead and calm the newcomers.

As the long row of boxcars rolled in day and night with new deportees, the musicians played classical music. SS soldiers[1] and *Kapos*[2] screamed, dogs barked, families separated, children cried, and men whispered. It was strange to hear the music.

Those musicians greeted victims to whom the symphony music was their last calming memory. It gave them some relief before they were murdered.

In the spring of 1944, in one month alone, about half a million deportees arrived. They came in large transports, especially from Hungary, the former Czechoslovakia, Serbia, and Romania's Transylvania. My family and I arrived from occupied Romania.

Since 1944, a question often comes to my mind about those who played music as new deportees arrived. Did any member of the orchestra survive the Holocaust? Did the musicians testify about their misery, experience, and the constant flow of boxcars that day and night brought innocent deportees to their deaths?

The musicians lived through their ordeal knowing the fate of every person who was directed to the left. Selection to the right meant temporary survival for about 1 to 2 percent of the new arrivals.

1. Nazi soldiers who were in charge of exterminating the Jews and other people who were considered inferior by the Germans.

2. Inmates, many of whom had criminal backgrounds, who were appointed as overseers of work teams and all other detainees.

SHOWER IN BIRKENAU

On Friday, June 2, 1944, we arrived in Auschwitz-II/Birkenau. What happened next was like a nightmare.

When our train of deportees arrived, we lined up in front of an officer. With a wave of his gloves, he decided who should live and who should die. My group was sent to the right. We were not yet condemned to die. But most from our transport were directed to the left. We had been locked up for seven days without water or food and we did not even have enough air.

Soldiers with rifles ready to shoot ordered us on the right to line up, five in a row; they held barking dogs on leashes. Men in striped uniforms helped the German soldiers group us. We walked on a road between barbed wire. Our group arrived at a big building. Our escorts screamed, "Go inside! Fast!"

We entered a large hall with benches around the wall and numbered hooks. On the wall were signs written in

German and in Hungarian: "Tie your shoes together."
"Remember your hook number, to find your clothes
quickly." How organized the Germans were. What a lie it
was. We did not know. None of us got our clothes back.
Our folded clothes were sent to German citizens as
bonuses.

Screaming soldiers watched us undress. Our heads were
shaved. In the shower, the water was boiling hot for one
second, and freezing cold the next second.

We were thirsty; we were hungry. We desperately
waited for nourishment. The Nazis said, "Food and drink
will be distributed after you shower." The Nazis laughed at
our misery. It was fun for them.

THE FIRST FOOD
IN
SEVEN DAYS

*S*even days had passed since that Saturday morning, May 27, 1944, when we were forced out of the ghetto. No food or water had touched my mouth. The first moisture my body received was from the shower on the morning of June 2, 1944. Someone put a tiny piece of soap in my hand, and on it was written JUDE SIEDE.[1] SS soldiers watched us enter the shower room.

While water poured on my head, I stuck out my tongue to swallow some drops. It did not matter if the water was hot or cold. My mouth was dry; my lips were cracked. The water felt as if it would rejuvenate my tired body. There were no towels to dry us.

Next, our group, five in a row, was ushered to a wet and muddy road surrounded with double barbed wire. There were watchtowers every few yards with soldiers ready to shoot. Screaming SS soldiers escorted us with rifles and barking German shepherds on leashes. We arrived in a plaza, *Lager C.* It was cold. We had clogs[2] on our feet, our bodies were covered only with rags — no underwear, socks, or jackets.

We stood five in a row until it got dark. It rained as if the sky was crying for all of us. On my shaved head and my back, it felt as if thousands of needles were sticking my body.

Late that day, our group was escorted into a barrack with no beds. In ours, Block 20,[3] it rained through the roof. Knee-high muddy water was on the ground. It was dark, crowded, and it was miserable. To keep ourselves warm, we stood close to one another.

Late at night, a large bucket of brown liquid was distributed, in which some barley floated. We were told, "Everyone, swallow three mouthfuls." It was boiling hot. The next person watched to make sure the other wouldn't swallow more.

I swallowed three large mouthfuls. It was bitter and so hot that it burned my mouth. But who cared? My body got some nourishment for the first time in a week.

We slept standing on our feet. We were exhausted. Slowly, morning arrived. The overseer ordered us to run to the latrine, wash our faces, and hurry for roll call. In a few weeks, many young women got sick. They were selected and taken away.

1. Jewish soap.
2. Shoes carved from wood.
3. The barracks in the camp were large, numbered trailers called blocks.

IN BIRKENAU,
MIRI SAVED MY LIFE

*O*ur nightmare continued. Our group walked between sections surrounded by barbed wire. *Lager C* was a section with thirty-two wooden barracks. Each barrack housed 1,000 to 1,200 females. At night, everyone tried to sleep crowded into three-level wooden bunks. We from the Saláj region of what is now a part of Hungary were housed in Block 20. It was cold and a rainy day.

Mud and about twenty inches of water pooled inside the barracks. The next morning, a miracle occurred. My name was called. From Block 18, the Block *Älteste,*[1] Miri Leichner arrived with a small group of females, but I did not recognize who called my name. There, with shaved heads and dressed in rags were two of my cousins, Violet and Eva, from the Bihor region.

I was transferred to Block 18 where my cousins were. They had arrived two weeks earlier. We slept like sardines

45

in a can — fourteen on a raw wood bed with splinters. We shared one blanket. *Lager C* was crowded. Twice daily during roll calls, SS soldiers assisted by *Kapos* selected 100 to 150 young women. We new arrivals did not know where they were taken. They disappeared, and no one ever saw them again.

Standing outside for hours at a time was difficult. It rained; it was cold. It was too much for my fifteen-year-old body. On Sunday, June 4, 1944, during roll call, I got dizzy. Everything grew dark. I fell to the ground.

When I opened my eyes, Miri, our Block *Älteste,* poured some water on my face and said, "Child, go inside the block." Miri saved my life. I was not selected that day.

My parents in heaven watched over my fate. Miri put me to work. With a piece of brick, I scrubbed the tall chimney's brick all day. Using my fingers, I covered the cement between the bricks with a white bleach gel.

More than one thousand young females lived in our block. Those who worked were permitted to walk; the others had to sit on the three-level bunks. Whoever was tall had to bend her neck.

There was no clean drinking water. We were hungry and thirsty. The water was yellow and rusty. But it did not matter that the water was not clean, that it was bitter and metallic. We were thirsty. Because I worked, I was allowed to walk. Everyone said, *"Kis kalyhas,*[2] bring water." So I carried water to the bunks all day long.

Sometimes, with a group of girls, we were sent to carry large canisters with food. Close to the distribution place, in the garbage, were piles of dirty potato peels. When the *Kapo* looked the other way, we filled our empty stomachs with potato peels. The dirty potato peels helped me to survive.

1. An overseer appointed by the Germans. Miri Leichner was the daughter of a rabbi from Bratislava, Czechoslovakia. I have spoken with her daughter, who lives in Australia.

2. Little kiln. In Hungarian, it sounds very nice, but the English translation does not sound so nice.

ROLL CALL
IN
BIRKENAU

*S*urrounded by barbed wire and in the shadow of four smoky chimneys, we reported to roll call twice a day. The first one began at daybreak and lasted a few hours. The second roll call started at midday and ended when the sun went to sleep. The *Kapos* let us go to eat and sleep when it was dark.

Our beds were large, made from raw wood, three levels on top of one another. Fourteen women slept on each level. When we moved, splinters stuck our bodies. Fourteen of us shared one blanket. We were like sardines in a can with no space between our tortured bodies. When one turned, all had to turn. We slept one head next to a pair of legs. We could smell the other person's feet. Our exhausted, weakened bodies could not take the misery for much longer.

We had only one dress to wear each, and our shoes were wooden clogs. Often it rained, so we got soaking wet. It did not matter that we were young. Many collapsed, and some fell ill. At every roll call, there were selections. The Nazis took the weak away.

The *Kapos* helped the Germans. They were collaborators. They knew the fate of those who were selected. The ones who were selected disappeared forever from this torment.

Wrong place,
wrong time

*I*t rained often in Auschwitz-II/Birkenau. It was terribly cold to stay outside in the rain for hours during roll call.

Many new arrivals with shaved heads caught colds. Some got diarrhea because of a lack of protein in the food. At the next roll call, they were selected and gone forever. Where were they taken? They disappeared without any trace.

Miri, our overseer in Block 18, took pity on us, the newly arrived inmates. Because of the heavy rain that day, Miri kept us inside the block. A group of SS came to count twice a day and select the inmates who looked sick.

A young Czech girl was responsible for us to be ready in time for roll call. Margo Grese was the head of the SS female soldiers. She came to count us, to select the sick or the healthy girls for the various medical experiments.

The Czech girl was scared and screamed, *"Schnell, schnell."*[1] With one hand, she hit any woman who was close to her reach.

Unfortunately, I was nearby. I got hit on my mouth. For a second, stars sparkled in front of my eyes. I was lucky, I received only one punch. On that day's roll call, I was not selected or beaten like other unfortunates. None of us did anything wrong; some were just in the wrong place at the wrong time.

1. Fast, fast.

A SLICE OF BREAD
AND A
DROP OF WATER

*I*n Auschwitz-II/Birkenau there were two daily roll calls. The first began before sunrise and lasted till midday, with the sun above our heads. The second roll call began after a short break and lasted until sunset. Then a one-inch slice of dark bread was distributed to each inmate. It was such a small piece, heavy and bitter. It had no nutritional value and was made from sawdust. We were so hungry that we did not feel the bitter taste. It was not enough to fill up our empty stomachs. Most inmates, as soon as they received the tiny slice of bread, stuffed it in their mouths and swallowed it on the spot.

The daily hunger created jealousy between inmates. Often the person who was ahead in line thought that the next one would receive a slightly thicker slice. It happened between friends and even relatives, so that miserable days turned even more distressing.

The water was not suitable to drink. It was rusty and yellow. But when one is thirsty, one will drink even mud. The water had a metallic taste, and many got diarrhea from it.

Food was another source of disease for the young women. A lukewarm, bitter, green soup with pieces of sand was given to us. Even though we were starving, we could not eat the green soup. We pushed it under the barbed wire to the Czechoslovakian Jews. Poor souls, they had been incarcerated for years in Terezin, the so-called family camp.[1] They arrived at Auschwitz-II/Birkenau with their families. They were only skin and bones, those starved skeletons eagerly waiting to receive the bitter green soup.

Now and then other lukewarm soup was given to us, in which floated pieces of yellow beets. In better days, we knew that animals were fed with the same beets.

It ran through our minds, *Could we just be dreaming?* It seemed so long ago that we had bread to eat and crystal-clear water to drink.

---

1. Also known as Theresienstadt, it was a special concentration camp that was part of the Nazi propaganda campaign to deceive the world into thinking that Jewish families were not separated or murdered.

Jews from Czechoslovakia

In the summer of 1944, the Jews from Theresienstadt arrived in Birkenau. They looked like ghosts. Men, women, and children were only skin and bones. Poor Jews, they had been starved for years in Theresienstadt. These skeletons hardly moved; their clothes were infested; their weakened bodies could not survive much longer.

Men in striped rags carried away the dead daily, loaded in two rows on a cart, their stiffened bodies on top of one another. Men, women, and children. The dead looked like wooden logs.

The few who lived a few more days ate the green bitter soup, the so-called food that was given to us in *Lager C*. Under the electrified barbed wires, we pushed the bitter, dirty, green soup through to the starving Jews from Theresienstadt.

Then one day, *Lager C* was closed. We had to stay in

our barracks, and the Jews from Theresienstadt disappeared. In the Czech *Lager,* there were no more starving, dying Jews.

When I asked an adult where they had gone, she said, "Don't worry, child. They were transferred to a warmer climate." I wondered how she knew where those Czech Jews were taken.

Every day for the last two months, I had seen the four tall chimneys pouring ash and fire into the sky, yet I had not realized in what kind of place I was.

Daily selection on roll call

At Auschwitz-II/Birkenau in *Lager C,* roll call was twice daily. It did not matter if it was rainy or sunny. We stood five in a row for hours, waiting for the SS officers to count us. Some of us, the temporary survivors of the first selection, became sick and passed out during roll call. Nazi SS selected 100 to 150 young women at the morning's roll call from our *Lager C.*

The SS came with rifles and barking dogs, screaming "dirty Jews." We had no water to drink, no water to wash ourselves. We were not considered human. We were less than animals, less than flies.

If one had a cold on the morning roll call, she was selected and disappeared forever. We, the most recently arrived from Hungary and other countries, were named by the Czech, Slovak, and Polish inmates *grine.*[1]

Every day I saw the four tall, smoky chimneys. The sky looked cloudy from the ash and smoke. I thought it was a

The only photograph of me (at the age of two)
that survived the Holocaust.

My brother, Adalbert, at age three.

My parents, Irina and Eugen Berkovits.

An example of the type of cattle car that carried deportees to Auschwitz-II/Birkenau and other concentration camps.

The "Death Gate" of Auschwitz-II/Birkenau.

The false message Arbeit Macht Frei
(which translates to "Work Makes You Free")
over the gates at Auschwitz-II/Birkenau.

Photo taken at the Auschwitz-II/Birkenau ramp on June 2, 1944. The small boy and the woman holding him are my mother and brother.

The orchestra at Auschwitz-II/Birkenau.

Suitcases of deportees murdered at Auschwitz-II/Birkenau.

Roll call at Auschwitz-II/Birkenau.

*The Volkswagen factory in Fallersleben, Germany,
where I was forced to work as a slave laborer.*

*Emaciated prisoners liberated on May 7, 1945, by Allied forces at
Ebensee, an Austrian concentration camp.*

*Photo taken on July 25, 1945, after liberation. I am
second from the right. My cousin Eva is second
from the left; Violet is on the far right.*

My wedding photo. I married Ernest Gross on June 24, 1946.

My son, Tiberiu, at age two, and my daughter, Agneta, at age eight.

My college graduation photo.

tire factory; it smelled like burned rubber. Years after the Second World War, I realized that those factories produced only death. There, innocent people were murdered. They were robbed, even after death, of their clothes, hair, and any other possessions they might have still had.

1. Pronounced green-eh, this Yiddish word, for the color green, was used for new arrivals.

We were naked

There was a selection on the last day of August 1944 in Auschwitz-II/Birkenau. It was conducted by Dr. Josef Mengele, the notorious "angel of death," who used humans as guinea pigs for all kinds of experiments. From Block 18, we were ordered to exit naked through the back door and enter into Block 16 at its back entrance.

On the road, armed soldiers with dogs and club sticks were assisted by *Kapos,* who made sure that no one should escape the selection. From Block 16, we exited through the front door.

There was Dr. Mengele. With his white gloves, he pointed some of us to the right, others to the left. My tummy was enlarged from the potato peels I had eaten with dirt and sand from the garbage dump. Dr. Mengele pointed to me. Vera, his assistant, asked, "Are you pregnant?"[1] I did not understand her. I answered, "I am fifteen years old." Dr. Mengele waved his gloves, so I passed his selection into the larger group. Years later, I realized how close I was to my last day.

Again Dr. Mengele separated sisters, mothers. They screamed, cried, and were brutally beaten. The group on the left remained between Blocks 16 and 18. We were naked, trying to warm one another. None of us witnessed it, but historians know that those selected to the left side were transported and murdered that day.

Our group was ushered to the disinfection building. After being disinfected, we received other rags and wooden clogs to wear, but no undergarments. But as our group approached the ramp, we were ordered to return.

The female officers escorted us into another *Lager*. There the fence was covered with blankets. Behind the fence, smoke rose from the ground. Occasionally, high, red smoky flames erupted. The strong smell of burned rubber was intense.

We were ordered to undress in the open yard. Our large group from *Lager C* stayed naked outside. The next day, we were ordered to get inside another block.

The rooms were small, and the floor was wood. The *Kapos* distributed pajama tops and a warm liquid to us. By a stroke of bad luck, I received pajama pants instead of a top, which I was not supposed to have. The *Kapo* who gave me the pants screamed and beat me to cover her mistake.

If the ever-present Nazi female guard saw me receive pants instead of a top, she would have punished the *Kapo*. To hide her mistake and to satisfy the Nazi officer, I was beaten. The *Kapo* gave me a punch that broke one of my teeth. My heart was so bitter that I did not feel pain.

1. Growing up as sheltered girls, we had never heard the word "pregnant."

Misery changes human behavior: some detainees' lives improve

*L*ife was miserable in the concentration camps. Those in the forced-labor camps were beaten, and most of the detainees were kept out in the open. For the prisoners of war, life was somehow better. It was more bearable than for those detained in the camps. Most detainees suffered hunger, infestation, beatings, and cold.

Human feeling disappeared for the majority of inmates who were incarcerated. Some detainees willingly collaborated with the Nazis. Sometimes I think that those who helped the SS were given drugs to behave so inhumanely toward us.

Jewish detainees were treated more brutally than non-Jewish prisoners of any other nationality. For example, before sunrise each morning, rain or shine, *Kapos* screamed at and beat the detainees of three blocks, ordering them to run into the wash trailer. In each block, there were about

1,000 to 1,200 women, yet detainees from three blocks had to squeeze into one wash trailer.

We had twenty minutes to wash our faces and use the latrine. There was no soap, towels, paper, or space. Then we ran to stand for roll call.

After a few months, my life changed again. I was selected to be shipped with a large group of detainees to a factory near Fallersleben, Germany. Here things were better. We had warm water with which to wash ourselves.

Each inmate slept in a single bunk bed with one blanket, a straw mattress, a straw pillow, and a semi-heated room with some lights. Compared to Auschwitz-II/Birkenau, this was a big change in our lifestyle, but we still had wooden clogs, one rag to wear on our backs, no undergarments, or change of clothes.

Each morning and evening, I ran to take a shower. The lukewarm water refreshed my tired body. We also had a toilet, but no papers or towels to wipe or clean ourselves.

Female officers counted us, then escorted us across the road to work. From the factory entrance, we walked deep down to a lower level and entered a large room with large machines. Six of us were put to work in a narrow hallway.

A GERMAN *MEISTER*
BROUGHT ME SALT

*O*ur group of five hundred from Auschwitz-II/Birkenau had arrived in Fallersleben on September 3, 1944. The next day, about half of us were escorted into the factory. Six of us were selected to work in the painting department. The material to be painted arrived on an assembly chain.

The material was a heavy round metal object with a handle. The oval top on its center had a six-angle screw with a diameter of about three inches and depth of an inch. It looked like a flower. On one side was a small hole where no paint was allowed. If paint accidentally leaked into the hole, one of the three *Meisters* complained to the female SS officers, who screamed at us. The paint was in large containers. Rubber hoses were hooked to them. With one hand, we pressed a pistol to spray paint, and with the other, turned a rotating tray attached to the table. The finished objects were hooked on the assembly chain, which rolled into the dryer room.

We worked in two groups, either for twelve hours during the day or for twelve hours at night. I worked the nights. My arms and back hurt. In front of us was a large fan. Above was a grate where people walked. We were given a mask, working gloves, a short jacket, and two cups of skimmed milk.

By October 1944, my mouth was bleeding from the paint fumes. Blood leaked on my chin, and I had nothing to wipe it. One *Meister,* a kind gentleman, risked his freedom and brought me a handful of salt. He said, "Little child, rinse your mouth twice daily with the salt." The bleeding stopped, but I contracted a gum disease. My gums shrank, and the roots of my teeth were exposed. It was painful.

In December 1944, I began to cough and choke up big lumps of paint. I had terrible pain in my back. Shivering with fever, I asked not to be sent to work. Our medical person was a dental technician. She roughly said, "Elly, you must go to work." Tears came to my eyes. It ran through my mind that when I went home, I would tell my parents that she was not nice to me.

With the blanket on my back, I walked out of her office, and the *Hauptscharführer*[1] with a club in his hand entered. A few girls were in the hallway. They curiously looked on. At that moment, another miracle happened to me. The high-ranking officer asked, "Are you sick, little child?"

Usually, if you were caught with a blanket on your back, you were beaten. The sick were sent away. They disappeared.

The officer called the *Lager Älteste*,[2] Brana Heller, and said to her, "Assign Elly to wash floors in the living quarters." From then on I was not exposed to additional factory fumes.

1. A high-ranking officer in the SS.
2. An appointee who assigned work.

My first craft
in
Fallersleben

*I*n Fallersleben, everyone got a cup and bowl; one's own spoon, too. The turnip soup was distributed hot. Each person had a single bed with a straw mattress. It was such a change after Auschwitz-II/Birkenau where we slept like sardines, had no water to drink, and the food was almost inedible.

In Fallersleben, life was much better. We had water to drink, a semi-heated room, and an indoor toilet, but we did not have toilet paper. We had a shower with lukewarm water morning and evening. There were no towels to dry ourselves. But our bodies dried fast. Then we stood in line for food.

Because I worked in the painting department, I had access to black and beige paint. I painted on a cup and bowl my name, flowers, and other designs. Our female overseer, Anne-Marie, observed this. She was a pretty blonde female officer who often counted and escorted us to work. The factory was across from our living quarters. With a smile, Anne-Marie said, "Elly, come here." I was terrified, ready for a blow. I was seldom punished, but I did witness others who were beaten. By not asking permission to paint my accessories, I was guilty.

Anne-Marie smiled. I closed my eyes, ready to be beaten with her ever-present club. She said, "Elly, paint a design on my cup."

Anne-Marie liked her name and the flowers I painted on her cup. The next day, she gave me a green sweater, white thread, and needle. Anne-Marie said, "Elly, sew designs on my sweater." Anne-Marie liked the design I made on her sweater, but I did not receive a reward or extra privilege for my work. I was a slave. I continued to work in the factory, but it gave me great satisfaction that I had created something.

THE FACTORY COMPLEX

In Fallersleben, the Volkswagen factory was in a large rectangular area. As I recall, the tremendous complex had many individual buildings connected by bridges. Under the bridge of each building, trucks transported materials and people into the factory. Production parts were transported from one end of a building to the other on an assembly chain and on gigantic cranes.

Large trucks arrived daily and carried the finished products to the harbor. Vessels were loaded and unloaded in the harbor. However, during the war the Volkswagen factory changed its products and its workers.

We were housed on the main floor in one of the factory buildings. Soldiers escorted us daily to work and back. In the section of the factory complex where I worked, auto parts were no longer made.[1]

In January 1945, four girls and I were escorted by a female soldier, Christine, to a nearby men's facility in

Laadberg. The camp in Laadberg was surrounded with barbed wire. In Laadberg, we altered garments for *Hauptscharführer* Hanz Johannes Pump. It was winter. Our bodies were covered with rags; we wore only wooden clogs on our feet. We did not have underwear, jackets, or socks. Yet the fresh air cleaned our lungs. The ground was powdered with freshly fallen white snow.

Once, in the sky, planes appeared. They looked like silver birds. Soldier Christine ordered us to walk fast, to return to the bunker. Often there were air raids. The factory did not stop its production during air raids. In our living quarters, it did not matter if it was day or night. We were ordered into the bunker as many as four to five times day and night. Due to lack of sleep, some factory workers were injured on the job.

1. Near the end of the war, the factory manufactured parts for V-1 and V-2 rockets. Prior to that, prisoners of war mainly repaired aircraft.

The oppressed revolted

In my childhood, I had always heard that Jews never revolted. Even my mother told me that when someone says something you don't like, try to walk away without saying anything. The Auschwitz-II/Birkenau uprising was not my accomplishment; I was not there to contribute to it. But I am proud to read about it and retell the story of the Auschwitz-II/Birkenau detainees who worked in the gas chambers and crematoria, and who revolted.

Sonderkommando[1] was the name of the group of men who worked in the crematorium. Their job was gruesome. Many did not wish to live and took sleeping pills to die. Their life was the most miserable work anyone could imagine. Every few months, the Nazis killed the men who worked there and replaced them with new arrivals.

One day in the fall of 1944, with the help of seven brave young women, dynamite was smuggled into Crematorium IV. The brave men who worked as the

Sonderkommando blew up Crematorium IV. We must remember how unimaginably brave they were.

After the revolt, Nazi soldiers murdered every man who participated. The young women who smuggled in the dynamite and the *Sonderkommando* who exploded it are among the most heroic people in our history. Of the seven women who smuggled the dynamite into the crematorium, two sisters survived by a twist of fate. Crematorium IV was destroyed beyond repair.

A small gas chamber still stands in Auschwitz-I. Auschwitz-II/Birkenau had four large gas chambers and crematoriums. Each gas chamber had the capacity to kill about 3,000 deceived innocents in twenty minutes. In Europe during the Holocaust, the Jewish population was almost completely destroyed in the factories of death. (One wonders who would have been the Nazi regime's next victims after the Jews were gone.)

Today in the ruins of Auschwitz-II/Birkenau, visitors can see that the walls of the gas chambers and crematoria were three feet thick, as if they had been built to be a fortress. During the Holocaust, transports arrived with deceived innocents from almost every European country. Upon arrival on the unloading platform, victims were herded to their last destination. The tired and hungry arrivals were told that food and water would be distributed after they showered. For many, this news was a relief after their difficult journey. They eagerly awaited their food, water, and shower.

The Nazis were masters at deception; the innocent victims calmly walked down the steps to the undressing room. The escorts were polite, even helpful. We, the few who survived, wonder how the Germans, one of the world's most civilized people, used scientific methods to murder millions of people. We later learned that the deadly gas used to kill people was not stored in the camp. Each new batch of gas was transported to the camp in a car with a red cross on it. The Nazi regime carefully deceived everyone. Few people knew the truth, and most did not care.

1. Groups of Jewish male prisoners who were young and in relative good health. Their job was to remove the bodies from the gas chambers (extracting gold teeth and valuables), and take them to the crematoria for final disposal.

ALLIED SOLDIERS ROLL IN

*A*nxiously, I was counting the days, even though I seldom knew the date or day of the week. It did not matter whether it was rain or shine. Twice a day in rags we stood on roll call for hours, waiting for the SS soldiers to count us. Each day, soldiers selected some girls and took them away. We never knew the fate of the selected ones.

The heavy smoke in the air made the sky gray. At night, new transports arrived. I heard children cry. There were days that some ran screaming into the barbed wire. They died instantly. Every day I hoped the misery would end and that I could go home to tell my parents what I had witnessed.

Often I thought, *Life is not fair.* I was only fifteen years old and got sick with no one to care for me. Daily there were air raids, and SS soldiers took us into the bunker. Then something changed. At the beginning of April 1945, female soldiers escorted our group of women to the railroad and ordered us into cattle cars. The train rolled, then halted. SS soldiers ushered us with rifles and dogs to a new *Lager* surrounded with barbed wire.

We entered the yard and met a group of girls. They were part of the large group selected at the end of August 1944 in Auschwitz-II/Birkenau. They were shipped to this place, Salzwedel, Germany. As we mingled, some family members were reunited. With great joy, I met my two cousins, Violet and Eva, who were still alive. However, now that we newcomers had arrived, food was scarcer than ever.

Suddenly, the SS soldiers disappeared. We did not know where they went or what would happen next. Then incredibly good news: On April 14, 1945, the sun began to shine brightly as Allied and American soldiers rolled through the gate. They said, "You girls are free." I didn't comprehend the word *free,* but other girls did. They sang and danced and said, "We will go home!" That I understood. "Home to my family. Yes! That's where I want to go."

WE GOT OUR FREEDOM
AND
RAN AWAY

The American and Allied armies liberated us on April 14, 1945. We were free to go anywhere. But how? We had no money, parents, or guardians to guide us. How could I return from Germany to my country and hometown? To my parents and brother? I was in Salzwedel, far away from my family.

The Americans and the Allies had given us our freedom. We were no longer slaves. But what was the next step? We still lived in infested wooden barracks in a camp. The Allies first loaded us on open trucks and moved everyone into the Salzwedel armory. They placed five girls in a room with single beds. We could walk and sleep when or where we wanted.

The armory was in a large area surrounded by trees, green fields, and benches. Once a day, food was distributed —

food for everyone. Someone gave my cousin two large raw potatoes. With a shard of metal, she scrubbed, rinsed, and put the potatoes in a pot to prepare a fresh meal for us.

I collected some dry branches and leaves for the fire. We found two bricks, placed them close to each other, and then rubbed two stones until they sparked. A small fire started between the two bricks. The aroma of boiling potatoes filled the area.

Suddenly a Jeep stopped, and two uniformed American soldiers walked out. They brought a can of meat, opened it, and poured the contents on our boiling potatoes. They put a whole can of meat in the pot. We were shocked! The can would have been enough for two more servings.

One of the soldiers brought two spoons and sat close to us on the ground. The soldiers were smiling and talking, but we did not understand what they were saying. We did not speak their language, English.

The three of us got scared. We ran away, leaving our food in the yard. We hid in the closet or under the bed. The two soldiers looked for us in every room. Probably they wanted to explain the situation. They wanted to feed us with nourishing food. This is the way we celebrated our freedom. We ran away.

Later that day, the two girls who were our roommates went to retrieve the food we had left in the yard. We shared the fresh food with our roommates. The five of us enjoyed a delicious meal of potatoes and meat, almost like we used to have at home. After that experience, we never again had the courage to cook, walk, or relax in the park on a bench.

The two American soldiers were young; who knows how our lives would have changed if we had remained with them? Some girls were not afraid to talk with soldiers, especially those girls who spoke some English. A few of them got married to American soldiers. They left Germany with their new husbands and moved to the United States.

Every day we woke up with the hope that somehow we would arrive home under our parents' protective wings and resume life the way it was before the war. We had not yet learned that our parents, brothers, sisters, and other family members were no longer alive, and that we were orphans.

I DISCOVER A
HEARTBREAKING TRUTH

*E*ventually, I arrived in my hometown with high hopes, thinking how good it was to arrive in my city, to be seeing my parents and brother in our home. From the train station, I ran through the streets. However, to my surprise, strangers lived in the house. No one seemed to know the whereabouts of my parents.

Later a man said, "Your mother was murdered on arrival in Auschwitz-II/Birkenau." Another man who had been drafted with Daddy into a forced-labor camp said, "Your father was burned alive in the spring of 1943." *Oh, no, no! Life cannot be so cruel. Both men must not be telling the truth.*

The ground moved under my feet. I lost my voice, my smile, my hope. Then in a dream, Mommy said, "Do not worry. My two brothers in South America will take you into their home." I wrote to my uncles, "What should I do?" My letter wasn't answered. In my dream, I asked for Daddy's advice. He said, "My three brothers live in South America. One of them will take you into his home." I wrote to them, "What should I do?" The three brothers never replied. None of my five uncles could take care of me. I did not know what to do or where to go.

City officials relocated the people who lived in my parents' house. But the empty rooms of my ransacked home scared me. I did not have a bucket to carry water from the well or a glass from which to drink. I had no one to give me food. Bitterly, I sat alone on the dirty wooden floor.

Then I was invited to the home of my parents' tenant, for a plate of soup and a bed in which to sleep. My name was embroidered on the bedcover's corner. Like turning on a light, the embroidery awakened a memory. When I was eight years old, Mommy had made that cover for me. I asked, "Is this the cover that Mommy made for me?" Sadly, the tenant lied, saying, "No, I embroidered your name on it."

The same thing happened at my best friend's home. Years ago, our mothers were good friends. It seemed so long ago; maybe it was just a dream. One night after returning from Germany, I was invited to my friend's home for dinner and a night's sleep. The pillowcase and the quilt cover in their guest room were light pink, imprinted with small white flowers and leaves.

Years ago, a girl would be given a dowry. Parents began buying dowry items for their child when she was young. My parents bought the pink material for me. Mommy trusted her friend and gave it to her for safekeeping. During the Hungarian occupation, everything was confiscated from the Jews. I asked my friend's mother, "Is this the material Mommy brought here?" My friend's mother denied it, saying, "Your mother never gave me anything." I could not force her to return the material; it already had been sewn into pillowcases and quilt covers.

I walked like a zombie in my hometown. My parents in heaven prayed for my well-being. Slowly I began to talk, but even today I think of my parents and brother with sorrow.

Long ago, I forgave my parents' five brothers who abandoned their orphan niece. The wind blew away my dreams to be with my family. Heartbroken, I survived alone.

MY HUSBAND'S STORY

I met my future husband, Ernest, after I returned to my hometown. This is his story and the story of others like him who lived in Hungary and other occupied countries during the war. In 1942, the Hungarian government drafted Jews between the ages of eighteen and fifty-five. Ernest was twenty-one years old. Young men were forced to work hard labor.

They were beaten. They slept outside in the snow without food or warm clothes. During the cold nights, some froze to death. From their original group, more than 90 percent did not survive the war. They were forced to walk on foot to Polish lands and into the Russian tundra. At the end of 1943, the German and Hungarian armies were pushed out of Poland and Russia.

The handful of surviving young laborers were forced by armed soldiers to retreat on foot to Hungary. Those still alive were placed in a shed in the city of Balf, on the

Austria-Hungary border. They suffered from typhus and high fevers for days. Ernest lost consciousness. When he awoke, he crawled out of the shed.

He remembered, "I rolled a stick on the blanket; the lice on it were as thick as the blanket. In a few days, we were forced to walk again. Those who could not walk were shot on the spot." This later was known as the Death March. Ernest continued, "Few survivors reached Austria's Dachau, Mauthausen, Gunskirchen, and Wels." [1]

Fortunately, the skeletonlike survivors were liberated by Allied forces on May 6, 1945. Slowly they went home. They had no family to whom to return, just empty homes. Every household had been ransacked. The handful of survivors worked hard. They tried to put their broken lives back together. The younger ones got married and raised families. Each survivor was marked by that hard time.

1. Concentration camps.

Coming to America

With tremendous effort, my husband and I moved to a large city, Oradea, in Romania. Our new home had a large garden. I dug holes in the backyard to plant forty fruit trees and in the front yard, thirty roses. With love, I watched how they grew. When they bloomed, it warmed my heart.

Unexpectedly, one day, we received visas to leave our native country, our city, our home, and our garden. The man who was to receive our home demanded some changes. To receive our visas, we were required by law to give away our home; we had to pay the city for any requested changes, such as painting the house. The city took possession of our property without giving us any compensation. Preparing to leave behind everything and everyone we knew, we gave away the key to our house.

We left our homeland for the unknown, with neither valuables nor money. Our two young children — our daughter, Agneta, and our son, Tiberiu—were all our wealth. We spent many sleepless nights in Italy, waiting six months to receive visas to enter the United States. Finally, we arrived in America on March 17, 1966. It was Saint Patrick's Day. Everyone was celebrating the holiday, but we still had worries and concerns. Where will we sleep, how will we feed our children? No language, no home; where do we go? What we will do?

With time, our worries passed. It did not matter that we worked sixteen hours a day. Our struggles gave our children a better life. Bless the day we arrived in the United States! America is the best country in the world.

OUR FIRST WORK
IN THE
UNITED STATES

*A*rriving in the United States, the biggest challenge was to find a job, in order to raise our two children. But in a new country, who would hire newcomers who didn't speak, read, or write English? In Italy, on the way to the United States, an organization gave us money for food, shelter, and lectures to learn English. Our children learned fast. But figuring out how to feed our children in the United States would not allow Ernest and me much time to concentrate on the lectures.

We were lucky when my husband's cousin greeted us at New York's JFK International Airport. He kindly gave us twenty dollars, a loaf of bread, a container of milk, a bag of potatoes, and dinner in their home for three days. And he arranged for us to sleep nearby.

We arrived on a Thursday. On Sunday, with two sub-way tokens and a piece of bread, I was sent to work in a factory. Using a sewing machine, I put together zip-out linings. The dust irritated the constant cough I had contracted in December 1944 when working as slave in Germany. It was like whooping cough; I choked and could not breathe. My new boss made me tea, and I continued working.

In ten days, I earned my first pay of thirty dollars. I felt rich. We went to the market and bought food for fifteen dollars. The children attended school and had lunch there. People advised us to ask the government for food stamps. But we were too proud to beg for assistance.

Our baggage arrived six months later. The children needed clothes. I bought remnant material for four dollars and sewed dresses for our daughter by hand.

In a few weeks, my husband got a dishwasher's job. Working without gloves, he washed dishes six days a week. The rough wire sponge irritated his soaked hands. At the take-out restaurant where he worked, there was plenty to eat, but the owner never offered him a bowl of soup.

Our road to create a living in a new land was difficult, but in spite of everything we made it. All we really needed was good health. We worked hard and were pleased that our fate brought us to the United States of America.

GOING TO COLLEGE

*I*n my youth, I had no chance for a higher education. When the opportunity finally came in America, I registered for college. My English wasn't the best, and my pronunciation was a disaster. In my first year, I had to repeat English class. For those of us born in foreign lands, it takes tremendous effort to learn how to speak and write English. In English, you do not read every letter and sometimes you pronounce them in different ways.

But I had learned; I was in college. Often I asked my professors for advice and help. Their encouragement kept me going. We live in the United States, in this beautiful country. If we don't understand English, we don't feel like real Americans.

Even though the textbooks were heavy, I carried them on the subway and bus. I sometimes felt miserable that none of my classmates invited me to do research together on the computer at the college library. Each semester, I took four classes in different subjects, desperately hoping to find a friend with whom to talk and study together.

Sometimes I invited a group of girls for coffee. I wished to be young; to have common ground with them for conversations; to laugh and to be a teenager. But I missed those years and had grown old at an early age. My youth was taken away from me.

Because of my other responsibilities, I had to study beginning at ten every evening until two or three in the morning. English, chemistry, and algebra were difficult, but I liked math, especially the Roman numerals, to which I had been accustomed since childhood.

It was hard to attend school in a new country with a much younger generation. But I made it.

POETRY

BY

Elly Berkovits Gross

Our Empty Home

*Today, I just turned fifteen; I felt
    so old, grown-up.
But when they ordered us to leave
    our home
I held my mother's hand and asked
    where would we go?*

*Mother was holding my brother's and
    my hands, but she could not say
    where we would go.
Mother embraced her trembling
    children's hands.*

*The door opened quickly and
    I remember first seeing a
    soldier's neck.*

*The order came, "Fast, get out fast
    from your home."
Quickly, we were ready to leave
    our home.*

Asking the question, "Misters, may I
take a bottle of water, and please
let me take a jacket for my five-
year-old son?"

Mommy was cursed, almost hit,
and she was called never-heard names.

The young man was from our street
with whom in earlier times we
climbed hills.

In our hands, nothing;
In our heart, love for one another
as we walked down our street.

Where Do We Go?

The sun was shining, but did
 not shine on us.
Mother, brother, and I left
 our lovely home.
Father had been drafted
 two years earlier.

A year later, only I returned to
 our empty home,
as a lonely child, with a
 broken heart.

There Is No Bird or Butterfly

Barbed wire with high voltage,
*   and watchtowers with soldiers.*
I can see only four tall chimneys
*   that pour ash and fire.*

The air is full of heavy smoke;
*   it smells like burned rubber.*
I can never see the sun because
*   the sky is blurry.*

When the sun shines, it is still
*   cloudy, and when it rains,*
*   the ground is muddy.*
I walk on sand and stone.
There is no grass or tree.

If some green would grow,
without any shame,
I would pick it to eat —
even at the risk of being killed.

I am enclosed with my
*   fellow inmates.*

Our crime is that we were born Jews.
This place is forgotten by everyone
   in the world.

The Nazis and collaborators
   robbed us of everything: our
   freedom, our possessions, and
   ultimately, our families' lives.

Our relatives are gassed, burned,
   their ashes thrown in the river.
We who were selected to the right
   are only temporary survivors.

Birds and butterflies never fly;
   they do not like smoke in the air.
I always wished to be a bird, so I
   could fly away.

To leave this sad place and go home
   to my parents.
But I did not have wings to fly
   like a bird or butterfly.

Please Come, Mommy. I Miss You.

Mommy, all my teeth hurt and my
mouth is always bleeding.
I am cold, where are you, Mommy?
I miss you, please come, Mommy, put
your hand around my shoulder,
kiss my cheek, my dear mother.
I am alone among strangers.

As soon as I see you, dear Mommy,
all my pain will go away.
My back hurts, I am cold and
shivering, come to me, Mommy.
Surrounded by strangers, no one
cares that I am alone,
I miss you, please come, Mommy.

Mommy, I have a fever, I am cold,
come to see me for a day or two,
put your hand on my forehead,
so the fever and pain will go away.
I ask adults, "Where is my mommy?"

"Please tell my mommy I miss her."

No one tells me where my mommy is.

Adults do not help or ask how I feel,
I have a sharp pain in my back,
Mommy.
I cough badly, and I am ready to
choke on large lumps of stinky
beige paint.
Come put your hand on my shoulder,
so I will stop coughing up beige
paint.
Each day I pray that you come to see
me, Mommy.

Mommy, I miss your hug,
your kindness, and your love.
Come to your daughter.
Please put your hand on my back and
forehead, so the pain will go away.

As soon as I see your lovely face, feel
    your kiss and touch on my forehead,
    all my sickness will go away.

Dear Mommy, when will you
    come to see me?
I am coughing loudly, it disturbs
    everyone and they complain,
    no one can sleep.
I am fifteen, a child. Please come,
    Mommy, help your daughter to
    get better, put your hand on
    my forehead, on my back, so all
    my sickness will go away.
I miss you, Mommy.

WHOSE SHOE WAS THE RED SANDAL?

In the large pile of leather shoes,
behind the unbreakable glass,
a red sandal is standing out in
the display.
Only one shoe, where is the other one?
Who wore that once good-looking
sandal?

Where is the other sandal from the
pair?
In this huge pile of victims' shoes
the other shoe is nowhere to
be found.
The owner is not searching for
her shoe.
Maybe she is long gone from
this world.

By fate she could have been selected
to the right, which meant a
temporary survivor.
Why did she never return to look
for her shoes?

Where did she disappear? Where did
  she go?
What was her fate? Did she suffer?

Who was the owner of the red sandal
  with the small white trimming?
  One can see it's a small size and
  once looked good.
She had to be young to have a red
  shoe.
Who knows were she was sent on
  arrival.

Was the girl's fate the gas chambers,
  or was she selected to the right
  which meant only temporary
  survival?
The long hours of roll calls, the food,
the smoke in the air, the daily misery.

Occasional beatings, our shaved
  heads,

our bodies covered with rags. Often it
  rained.
It felt like a thousand needles stuck
  our bodies.
Many got sick. The Nazis calculated
  that a healthy person would
  survive six months.

On arrival, at the first bath, we
  placed our belongings under
  numbered hooks. None of us got
  our clothes, shoes, and other
  belongings back.
They were packed and shipped as
  bonuses into Germany.
For these shoes on display, the time
  ran out.

The Russian army liberated the
  camp. The Nazis could not ship
  the piles of victims' shoes.

*They remained as witnesses of the
 Nazi era.
The red sandal with white trimming
 stands out in the display. Where is
 its owner?*

Our Daughter

When she was born,
I put a red bow in her long
  auburn hair.
She had a round face and
  beautiful blue eyes.

When she did not cry, I would
  think that she was a doll
  from a store or a display in
  a museum.

When she was nine months old,
  she walked, and she balanced
  her fragile body with her
  small hands.

She was pretty, smart, and always
  asked questions.
Why are leaves green?
Why does water have no color?
Why is the milk white?

Her questions never stopped.
At the age of four, she read tales
   from books.
When she was five, she attended
   the first year of school.

She remembered every book she read,
   without looking into the book.
She was born witty and very pretty.

While I walked with her,
   people stopped to look at
   her beautiful face.
I was proud to have such
   a pretty child.

She grew to be a successful woman,
   a wife, the mother of two,
   and remains a loving,
   pretty daughter to us.

Four Seasons

"Spring is here."
The sun shines, and warms
     Mother Earth.
Meadows change color;
     new grass makes them green.
In the sky, wild geese fly, assure
     us that spring has arrived.
Birds are busy repairing or
     building new nests
     for their chicks.

In a few weeks,
     the weather gets warmer,
     nights are shorter,
     and days get longer,
     telling us, "Summer is here."
In rainbow colors,
     flowers are blooming.
Birds are busy feeding,
     and teaching their
     new chicks to fly.

"Autumn brings breezes,"
   and days are getting shorter.
Hills are filled with fruits,
   and birds prepare to fly away
   to warmer places.
Soon the weather gets cooler
   and rain changes to snow.

Meadows and forests
   are covered with a
   white blanket.
"Winter has arrived."
It puts nature to sleep,
   until the next spring.

Nature never gets old;
   the cycle is repeated,
   year by year.

My Hopes and Dreams

My Hopes Are:

Health to my family and to us as old parents.

Success for my children and to see them happy.

My Dreams Are:

Peace on Earth, especially in the United States and in the State of Israel.

People never should be hungry. No one should be homeless.

All terrorists should resign. There should be no more destruction of buildings, no more car bombs.

I worry when I watch the news; often I would rather not listen. It hurts to hear that daily, somewhere in the world, many parents, spouses, and children lose their loved ones to terror. We who lived through the Second World War feel the pain of everyone who has lost a family member. For families, it is painful when old age or sickness takes one's life away. Family members mourn for the loss of the departed, and forever they will keep the memory in their hearts. Tragedy hits every family who loses a loved one by accident or terror. A deep hole remains in the family's heart that never entirely heals. The close relatives smile with tears in their eyes and with pain in their hearts. Family members can seldom truly laugh.

My Other Hopes Are:

To win the lotto to build an old age home for those who can't afford an aide to help them and to build a home for orphaned children.

My Other Dreams Are:

*To live in good health, never to need
others' assistance for the existence of
my everyday life.*

The Time I Was a Child . . . Maybe

These childhood memories reflect a
worry-free, short childhood.
They are from the years 1936 and
1937, they are from the years
before the cloudy sky fell on Jews.
They are from the years before the
Hungarian invasion of Romania
on September 10, 1940.

On our street, eight of us had a sort
of friendship.
Four girls and four boys. After school,
we played together.
Summers we climbed the hills to
pick berries or wildflowers,
mushrooms or chestnuts to take
home to our mothers.

Winters we were on the ice. The cold
did not bother us.
The friendship was only on the street
or on the hills.

Our parents never would permit us to
play in the house.
Rainy days were boring, especially on
Saturday afternoons.
Some Saturday mornings, I went to
visit Klari and play with her.
She lived on our street with her
mother, Sari, and her aunt Berta.
Klari was my smart, pretty classmate,
who played the violin.
Her father and her twin sister died
many years before.

Klari never came to play on the street
or climb the hills.
I played with her in their home.
Mother allowed two hours
but while we were busy playing, I
often lost track of time.
Because I got home late, for a few
weeks I had to stay home.

Eagerly I awaited the Saturday I
    could play again with Klari.
School was six days a week. Relief
    came on Saturday
when there was more fun.
Those happy days did not last for
    long; life became harsh.

The children on the street abandoned
    me and called me names.
So-called friends never noticed me, I
    was very lonely.
On warm summer days I was not
    invited to climb the hills, collect
    berries, or pick wildflowers.

Nor on cold winter days to sled, build
    snowmen, or throw snowballs.
Time and mood had no space to a
    Jewish child. We children grew old
    early; life became harsh and

miserable. In a short time,
the wind blew everything away.
Everyone's hopes and dreams
vanished.

Jewish lives were changed, destroyed,
and wiped out.
On arrival in hell, at Auschwitz-II/
Birkenau, Dr. Mengele, with a
wave of his gloves, decided who
should live, who should die.
Klari's aunt Berta did not pass the
selection.

Then in July of 1944, in Blocks 14 to
28 the 1,000 to 1,200
female inmates in each block were
lined up naked. Klari and her
mother did not pass this selection.
As had many others, they
disappeared forever.
For how long was I a child?

Those with Sore Throats Disappeared

My life as a slave began in 1944 at Auschwitz-II/Birkenau, where seldom could one meet someone from the previous life. Never was sure if I had a bad dream or if Mommy would say, "Wake up, get ready for school."

In about July 1944, in *Lager C*, running to the latrine, I met my parents' best friend's daughter, Iboly, a beautiful young girl. I was joyous to see her, I pinched my arms — that pretty girl was really Iboly. She looked miserable, pale in a torn dress, with a rag around her neck. I asked, "Iboly, why do you have that rag on your neck?" She said, "My throat hurts, the rag keeps it warm." Iboly was the best-dressed girl in our city, pretty and chic; her brother Alex, a textile salesman who traveled, bought rare materials for his sister; their mother made elegant garments for Iboly.

In the 1930s, Iboly's father was a carpenter in the United States, who saved money and then returned to his family. He bought a modest house and continued to work as a carpenter. In the ghetto, Hungarian soldiers presumed that he hid valuables; he was tortured and died of his wounds.

Next morning, I wished to find Iboly again, but could not. In *Lager C* the barracks had 30,000 detainees. Twice daily we had roll calls that lasted a few hours; four blocks of detainees had a half hour to use the latrine and washroom. It was very crowded.

On daily morning roll calls, Dr. Mengele selected the sick and the blondes. Iboly had a sore throat and was blonde. I asked where they were taken. An adult said, "Do not worry, the sick get medical help and the blondes get a special task." Mommy always said, "Respect and believe the elders."

As I think of Iboly and others who faced the same fate, it naturally comes to my mind to ask how the catastrophe on Jews had been invented by the most civilized people on our Earth. How was it possible that with advanced science, they murdered millions? The world was silent.

In August of 1945, I returned home and met Iboly's brother, Alex. He asked, "Elly, do you know where my sister is? Did you meet Iboly?" I began to cry for Iboly, for my parents, my brother, relatives, friends, and everyone who disappeared from my life. I had no home where

I could go; for days I could not talk and walked about like a zombie.

Alex survived hell alone and left the country. At the border he was killed; the family had no other survivors. The question comes to me again why a young, beautiful girl, for a sore throat, disappeared forever.

Thank you for the welcome in your
lovely home, as I was greeted
by you.
My life was shadowed by heavy
storms, which I remember with
tears in my eyes.

My life was rough and tough, even
though I have been my father's
single sunshine, my mother's
only child, whom she dressed in
pink or blue with a bow in my
blonde hair.

Neglected by my friends, I felt lonely.
I was ten, when a miracle happened
and I got a handsome little
brother, with red cheeks, black eyes
and hair; I loved him a lot.

Cruelty of life took away all of them.
No one called me "my dear
sunshine," or said, "my dear girl,

come inside, a storm will soon
arrive and you could catch
a cold."
The little brother with open arms —
and with a smile on his face — did
not walk again toward me to grab
my arms.
With sorrow I miss them as long as
I live.

With tears, I ask why I lost my
loved ones.
Almost at the sundown of my life,
I found a lovely cousin, who took
me in her arms and home, like
the sister who I never had.

Silent World!

In my childhood, Gentiles called me
"Stinky dirty Jew, go to Palestine."
I often washed my white skin,
but for Gentiles I remained dirty.

When I complained, Mommy said,
"You, my child, must learn not
to complain, but take it as it is."
While being a slave, I remembered
not to complain of daily miseries.

Seven miracles came on my way
to surviving the massacre of
European Jews.
Miracle eight didn't come on
my way; one of my parents
should have survived, as a lonely
child I alone survived.

In memory of my parents, I plant
flowers every year and remember
Mommy's small garden where
    flowers bloomed and filled the
    air with fragrances.

Most broken objects could be glued,
    but my broken heart never healed.
With sorrow I remember the bitter
    past that took away so many
    innocent lives.

And I ask, Why did it happen?
In our civilized world, why did men
    in blind hatred turn to evil?
And why was the world silent?

On top of a tall tree, a bird family
 has a nest.
There are Papa, Mama, Sue, and
 Bob Bird. One day, Papa was
 called with many others to
 report to the bird center.
As many others birds,
 Papa Bird never returned.

Soon every bird was summoned;
 Mama, Sue, and Bob Bird with
 all the other birds arrived at the
 center. It was very crowded.
Sue Bird got lost, Mama and Bob
 Bird disappeared.
Desperately Sue looked for Mama
 and Bob Bird, but could not
 find them.

Suddenly the sky got dark and a
    heavy storm came that destroyed
    every bird nest. Fallen trees were
    everywhere.
Sue Bird never found Papa, Mama,
    and Bob Bird.
With open wounds and torn feathers
    she flew from tree to tree looking
    for her family.

Sue Bird called: "Papa, Mama, Bob,
    where are you?
"How can I find you?" But she never
    found them.

While Sue was flying from tree to
    tree, she found a lonely bird with
    many wounds and torn feathers.
The two hurt birds built a nest on top
    of a tall tree, which stood in spite
    of heavy rain and wind.

The two birds with open wounds and
*   torn feathers managed to raise two*
*   little birds,*
And now on top of the tall tree,
*   there again are four birds.*

They remember those birds lost in the
*   heavy storm and they are happy*
*   that even with their torn feathers*
*   and many wounds, they raised*
*   two new little flying birds.*

Author's Note

When the war ended in 1945 and I learned that my family had perished, I made a firm vow to myself to always write and talk about my tragic past, the Holocaust that I had witnessed and lived through.

So, in March of 1995, when a representative from the Shoah Visual History Foundation contacted me to get my testimony on the Holocaust, I was more than willing to speak about my experiences.

The Survivors of the Shoah Visual History Foundation was established in 1994 by Academy Award–winning director and producer Steven Spielberg. Mr. Spielberg founded this organization shortly after he directed the film *Schindler's List*. The Foundation's goal was to record videos of as many living Holocaust survivors as they could find. I was one of these survivors, and a representative arrived at my home in 1995 to record my recollections. In 2006, the Shoah Foundation partnered with the University of Southern California, and is now known as the USC Shoah Foundation Institute for Visual History and Education.

Today, this special organization still works to combat prejudice and bigotry in the world.

In 1998, I received a phone call from an attorney named Deborah Sturmann, who worked at the law firm of Milberg Weiss. Ms. Sturmann had watched the Foundation's video and wanted to use my testimony in a lawsuit her firm was bringing against Volkswagen. The firm charged that Volkswagen (and other German companies such as Audi) had used slave labor during World War II, and owed the survivors who had worked there reparations (payment).

I couldn't believe I had been asked to participate in such a groundbreaking case. Growing up, I'd been taunted by others and called a "dirty Jew." Now, in my advanced age, I was granted the privilege and the honor to allow my testimony to be used for a reparation trial. To this day I am filled with pride and satisfaction that my words helped many former slaves eventually receive a settlement. My involvement in the Volkswagen case was featured on the CBS program *60 Minutes*.

Though I received payment as well, I did not wish to keep the money. When the first settlement payment came to me, my husband and I paid for six orthopedic beds at Rambam Hospital in Haifa, Israel, in memory of our parents and families who were brutally extinguished in the prime of their lives. When there was a second payment, my husband and I forwarded the money on to Beth Halochem in Haifa, a rehabilitation center for wounded soldiers and civilians.

We hope for a better world. People should live in peace and harmony; there shouldn't be bloodshed between nations. It is very sad that innocents, especially children, suffer because of war. People must learn that hatred and prejudice create only destruction; at the end, there are no winners, only losers. I hope people will take my message to heart.

Afterword

Elly Berkovits Gross, my mother

I was lucky to be born ten years after Mother came back from the concentration camp. She was not very healthy when I was born; she had a severe respiratory infection. I later learned that she had worked as a slave in a factory plant. My sister also became severely ill when I was two years old, so Mom had to be away for months with her at the hospital. After my sister got better, we moved to the city, and I led a sheltered life. My family loved me and took care of me.

I was ten years old when my family moved to the United States, and for years I saw my parents very little. They worked at two, three jobs and went to night school to learn English.

Mother continued in school and proceeded to get her high school diploma. Then she took more courses so she would be able to get an office job. She was always trying to better herself and help her family prosper. She encouraged

Dad to start a business and left her office job to help him. My parents' hard work encouraged me by example and enabled me to get an education.

I am very proud of my mother's accomplishments. She is a great inspiration not only to me, but to all young people. Having been orphaned at the age of fifteen, she managed to create a good life for her family. But that was not enough for her. She now wants to leave a legacy and try to change the world. By letting people read about her experiences, she teaches them what discrimination leads to. She not only gives her time when she speaks in schools all over the country about her experience and against prejudice, but donates all proceeds from her books to charity.

My mother is a special woman.

— *Tiberiu A. Gross*